Brad Has a List

by Alejandro Sanchez
illustrated by Luanne Marten

Practice Decodable 22

McGraw Hill Education

Bothell, WA • Chicago, IL • Columbus, OH • New York, NY

MHEonline.com

Send all inquiries to:
McGraw-Hill Education
8787 Orion Place
Columbus, OH 43240

ISBN: 978-0-02-144762-6
MHID: 0-02-144762-4

Printed in the United States of America.

7 8 9 CTM 23

Brad has a big list.

Brad has some nuts and mints.

He grabs some cans and buns.

Brad likes lots of ham, clams, and jam!

Brad must have a mop and pans.

Brad drops bags, cans, and pans.
Brad must have some help!